Here Today, Here Tomorrow

Helping schools to promote attendance

by **Susan Hallam and Caroline Roaf**

Calouste Gulbenkian Foundation, London 1995

Published by Calouste Gulbenkian Foundation
98 Portland Place
London W1N 4ET
Telephone: 0171- 636 5313

© Calouste Gulbenkian Foundation
First published 1995
Reprinted 1997

ISBN 0 903319 71 3

British Library Cataloguing-in Publication Data
A catalogue record of this book is available from the British Library

Designed by The Upper Room 0181- 686 4414
Distributed by Turnaround Publisher Services Ltd 0181- 829 3000

Susan Hallam is a lecturer in the Department of Educational Psychology and Special Educational Needs at the Institute of Education, London University. She trained as a violinist at the Royal Academy of Music after which she spent ten years as a full-time professional musician. An interest in psychology led her to take a BA in Psychology externally with London University. This was followed by a career in teaching. She has written publications relating to truancy and exclusion from school, creativity, motivation, and the learning and performance of music.

Caroline Roaf has been a special educational needs co-ordinator in secondary schools in Oxford since 1979. During 1993/94 she held a part-time lectureship in the School of Education at Oxford Brookes University and was a research associate with OxSpec, an Oxford Brookes/ Oxfordshire LEA research initiative. She has a particular interest in how agencies co-operate to provide a network of support for young people whose needs are such that no single agency on its own can accept full responsibility for them. As a result of this interest, she was involved with the setting up of the GEST funded Oxford Attendance Project and became its co-ordinator, and was from 1989-94, convenor of the Oxford City inter-agency project Children and Young People in Difficulty (funded from 1992 by the Joseph Rowntree Foundation).

Acknowledgements

The authors would like to thank Simon Richey (Assistant Director, Education, at the Calouste Gulbenkian Foundation, UK Branch), Chris Watkins (Chair of the steering committee, Senior Lecturer and Tutor in Pastoral Care, Institute of Education, London University), Professor Hazel Francis (Emeritus Professor of Educational Psychology, Institute of Education, London University), Christine Peters (Head Teacher, Parliament Hill School), Deborah Cooper (Project Reseacher) and Yvonne Reynolds (Head Teacher, Earlham Junior School) for all their support and guidance; and also give grateful thanks to Chris Bradley (Educational Psychologist, Education Service Bedfordshire) and Elspeth Ferriday (Principal Education Social Worker, Oxfordshire) for commenting so helpfully on the text.

The research on which this booklet is based was funded by the Calouste Gulbenkian Foundation. Susan Hallam (project director) and Deborah Cooper (project researcher) would like to thank all the LEAs who participated: Barking and Dagenham, Barnet, Bedfordshire, Bradford, Brent, Calderdale, Cambridgeshire, Carlisle, Cheshire, Coventry, Croydon, Cumbria, Derbyshire, Devon, Dudley, Durham, Ealing, East Sussex, Gloucestershire, Hackney, Harrow, Humberside, Isle of Wight, Kirklees, Leeds, Leicestershire, Northamptonshire, North Yorkshire, Oxfordshire, Salford, South Tyneside, Southwark, Staffordshire, Stockport, Sunderland, Waltham Forest, Wigan, Wolverhampton.

Foreword

This booklet is designed to help schools promote good attendance. There are many reasons why pupils fail to attend school regularly. One important reason is anxiety about a particular aspect of school life, for example, the threat of being bullied, the strain of an over-competitive atmosphere, or a difficult relationship with a teacher.

Getting these aspects of school life 'right' is what constitutes a good school ethos. This is the point of connection between this booklet and the funding priorities of the Gulbenkian Foundation's Education Programme, which in recent years have focused on helping to improve the ethos of schools.

It is also worth stressing a point which is sometimes overlooked when the much-debated issue of school attendance is raised. This is that if pupils fail to attend schools regularly their education will suffer, which in turn will restrict the opportunities open to them once they have left school.

We hope that this booklet, which has been written for teachers, will prove helpful and supportive.

Simon Richey
Assistant Director, Education
Calouste Gulbenkian Foundation, UK Branch

Contents

Introduction

Truancy is not new. Since the education of children became compulsory, it has often been the focus of political and media attention. Recently, it has been portrayed as a major cause of social problems to be eradicated at all costs. To this end schools are now required to publish figures for authorised and unauthorised absence. These are reported in the press and scrutinised and commented on by politicians and the general public. To try and improve attendance some schools have introduced electronic registering systems. There has been a demand for pupils to wear school uniform so they can be easily identified. Truancy watch schemes, which involve schools, LEA education welfare officers, the police and local businesses, have been developed to promote greater community awareness of the problem. These usually focus on shopping centres where truants tend to gather. While most of the attention was initially directed at secondary school level, the scope has now widened to include primary schools. Through Grants for Education Support and Training (GEST), the government has provided funding to develop initiatives to improve attendance.

Is this level of concern justified? The reality is that most pupils go to school on a daily basis and enjoy it. According to a recent study,[1] 88% of pupils are "usually happy" at school, 70% say they work as hard as they can and report getting on well with most or all of their teachers, and over 50% report seeing their school as a 'good friend' or 'friend'. But, when asked about attendance at school, 17% of year 10 pupils and 20% of year 11 pupils reported playing truant. Even amongst the 11 year olds in year 7, 8% claimed to play truant, sometimes or often. For a proportion of the school population there does appear to be cause for concern.

Because truanting takes many forms, the direct effects of unauthorised absence from school are difficult to establish. Some pupils will occasionally absent themselves from lessons that they dislike. Others will be absent consistently over long periods of time. Certainly, persistent absenteeism from school can have adverse effects. Data from the National Child Development Study[2] has shown that there is a relationship between poor attendance at school, for any reason, and performance in reading and mathematics. In the long-term, persistent truants also tend to have lower status occupations, less stable career patterns and greater unemployment in comparison with others sharing similar backgrounds.[3,4] Some, but not all, truants may be involved in delinquency.[5,6]

The Elton report on Discipline in Schools[7] (1989) indicates that truancy not only damages the educational progress of the truanting pupil but can affect other students. They may be neglected while teachers help truants to catch up with work. Persistent absentees may also influence other pupils to follow suit. In lesson time, the presence of unsupervised pupils on school premises may undermine a productive working climate. Finally, if staff and the school are seen as not attempting to maximise attendance this transmits a negative, if unintended, message to pupils and parents alike, ie that teachers do not care whether pupils attend or not.

The future for young people is changing rapidly. The nature of employment is being transformed by the implementation of new technology and global economic factors. Young people need to achieve higher educational levels than at any time in the past. Non-attendance at school, even for short periods of time, may jeopardise their future opportunities by limiting their educational experience. While parents have a legal responsibility to ensure that their child receives efficient full-time education according to their age, ability and aptitude, schools play a fundamental role in ensuring good patterns of attendance which will enable every child to fulfil their potential in this fast changing environment.

If it is important that children go to school, why don't they attend?

❏ Some children may be prevented from attending school.

❏ Some children may wish to avoid school as it creates severe anxiety for them.

❏ Some children may simply not want to go to school.

This booklet explores these possibilities focusing on the ways that schools may develop practices to improve attendance. It is based on a nationwide survey of schools and LEAs funded by the Calouste Gulbenkian Foundation. The booklet draws together, from these findings, a range of successful practices for improving and managing attendance. Some of these are well established, others are new. The survey revealed that truancy is complex and requires careful and thoughtful consideration. There are no simple 'quick fix' solutions. It is necessary for each school, as part of its development plan, to consider the characteristics of its own school community and to adopt appropriate strategies to encourage pupils to attend.

The first section considers the difficulties in establishing the scale of the problem and outlines possible reasons for absence from school. Illustrations from recorded case studies are provided to demonstrate the complexity and diversity of non-attendance. The second section, based on evidence of good practice in schools, considers what can be done to promote attendance.

Centre of attention: PC Nigel Jackson and welfare officer Nigel Ross in Hanley's main shopping area

Blitz
trua
aim
cut

by

The Go
lions of
its thes
dards,
youn
crim

Mi

'Shouldn't you
be in school?'

TRUANTS
BEWARE

Bid to prevent
children from
ping school

Gerald
which l

Wh
co

by t

IT'S 8.30
early, Th
shows th
nary tu

Minu
used t
gradu
arcec
T
trua

Why don't pupils attend school?

Why don't pupils attend school?

In the extensive literature which has grown up around the issue of truancy, the causes have variously been laid at the door of the pupil, the family, the community and more recently, the school. It is now generally accepted that truancy is multi-faceted.

What is the scale of the problem?

The difficulty of obtaining accurate information

The extent of truancy is very difficult to establish, in part because there are no clear definitions of exactly what constitutes truancy or unauthorised absence.

It is relatively straightforward to assess whether a child has attended school by reference to official school registers. However, overall attendance figures do not enable **individual** patterns of absence to be identified. For instance, two schools may have an 88% average attendance rate. One may have high average attendance from the majority of pupils with a small minority of regular absentees reducing the overall rate. The other may have a fairly consistent attendance rate across the whole school.

Schools play a role in interpreting the Department for Education and Employment (DFEE) guidelines, particularly in relation to special occasions and what constitute exceptional circumstances within the categories. This makes meaningful comparison between schools impossible.

A further problem is post-registration truancy, where pupils attend for registration but then 'bunk off' selected lessons.

These difficulties make it impossible to produce reliable figures for unauthorised absence from official school records.

Researchers have used alternative information provided by parents, pupils or Education Welfare Officers (EWOs), sometimes known as

Educational Social Workers, in attempts to establish the extent of unauthorised absence. Such sources also pose problems. Parents may not be aware of their child's absence or may be afraid of admitting it for fear of court action. Pupils themselves may also find it expedient to minimise their absence or if they are guaranteed anonymity from officialdom may exaggerate to impress peers. Research based on information from Education Welfare Officers has also adopted different criteria to define unauthorised absence making comparisons difficult.

Given these problems, it is not surprising that the rates of attendance recorded in different research projects vary.

The overall picture as we know it

Recent figures for attendance at schools in England in 1994-95, published by the DFEE, suggest an overall 94% attendance rate in primary schools and 91% in secondary schools.

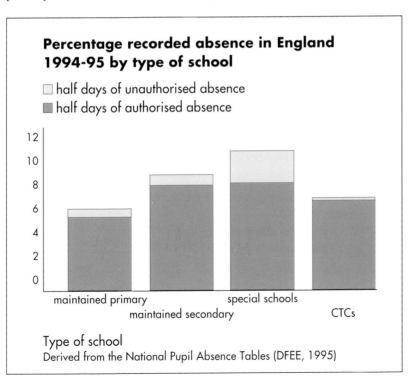

Percentage recorded absence in England 1994-95 by type of school

☐ half days of unauthorised absence
■ half days of authorised absence

Type of school
Derived from the National Pupil Absence Tables (DFEE, 1995)

These overall figures tell us very little about detailed patterns of absence within schools. Research undertaken in 150 schools drawn from 20 Local Education Authorities[8] in 1991/2 showed an 83% overall attendance rate of pupils in years 10 and 11 on the days of the survey. Data was collected, by questionnaire, directly from pupils. The study estimated both blanket truancy (taking whole days off from school) and post-registration truancy (skipping single or several lessons). The table below illustrates the overall findings.

Percentage of pupils in years 10 and 11 reporting differing levels of absenteeism

Levels of absenteeism	Percentage of pupils
Never truanted	69
Less than once a month	12.2
Once a month	4.7
Two or three times a month	5.4
Once a week	3.5
Two to four times a week	3.2
Every day	1.5

Of those engaged in truancy 64% claimed that they were involved in blanket truancy and post-registration truancy. A quarter of year 11 pupils reported missing lessons without leaving the building.

Despite the problems in obtaining accurate measurements a number of trends have been observed.

At primary level absence is highest when children begin school, improves in the middle years and then deteriorates again.[9]

Children with significantly higher than average absence at primary school are likely to be poor attenders at secondary level.[10]

There is an increase in absence as pupils transfer from primary to secondary school.

There is a general increase in absence as pupils progress through secondary school.

Unauthorised absence is highest in years 10 and 11.[11]

In all phases girls are absent more than boys, although there is little difference in their rates of unauthorised absence.

Friday is the most popular day to be absent from school.

Difficulties in establishing the extent of unauthorised absence apply within individual schools. In any institution, overall attendance is widely accepted as an indicator of morale. The best approach therefore, may be to consider overall attendance rates.

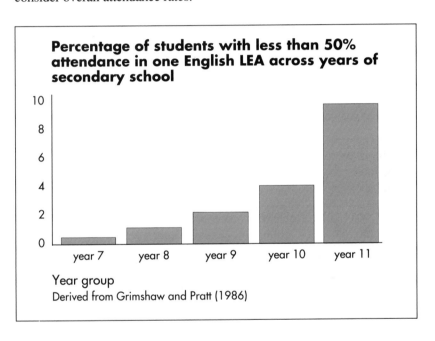

Percentage of students with less than 50% attendance in one English LEA across years of secondary school

Year group

Derived from Grimshaw and Pratt (1986)

Reasons for non-attendance at school

Illness and anxiety

The reason most often given for absence from school is illness. This is legally acceptable and on the surface seems simple and uncontroversial. However, appearances can be deceptive.

Minor illnesses such as colds will be viewed in differing lights by different families. Some children will be sent to school even though their work may be quite severely affected by a cold. Other children will be kept at home for illness which is minimal.

Patterns of attendance broken by a series of regular hospital or dental appointments can also lead to truancy. The opportunity to miss lessons legitimately establishes a pattern of non-attendance, which may be continued even when the appointments are no longer required.[12]

John is seven. He was happy at infant school but on moving into the junior department he found the work much more difficult. His anxiety was increased by a teacher, who he perceived as being unsympathetic. She seemed to be constantly telling him off and shouting at him. He worried about going to school, often waking in the night. In the morning he would complain of stomach pains or headaches. At first his mother was sympathetic and allowed him to stay away from school. She then began to suspect that anxiety was the problem and tried every means that she could to persuade him to go to school. His response was to scream that he was not going. If taken to the school he would kick and shout and have to be brought home or he would run off into the nearby woods. His behaviour changed almost overnight when a new teacher, who he perceived as being more sympathetic, took over his class.

Parents who are trying to get their child to attend school may feel unable to share their concern with teachers.

Teachers may be unaware that their behaviour can provoke anxiety in children.

The transition between phases of schooling or schools can be particularly stressful for pupils.

Illness can be precipitated by anxiety caused by stressful situations. These may occur at school. Children and adults commonly react to general stress by producing genuine physical symptoms. These often cannot be traced to any physiological cause.

For parents, deciding whether their child is genuinely ill or not can be problematic. Even if parents recognise that anxiety is the underlying cause, they may still justify absence in terms of illness. It is not surprising that children may also try to legitimise school absence in these terms. Research has shown that 27% of primary aged children have at some time pretended to be ill to avoid school.[13] Once stress is alleviated in this way the child is likely to repeat the action on subsequent occasions. In children there is also considerable overlap between not wanting to go to school and psychosomatic illness. One study of recurrent abdominal pain in children could find physiological organic causes in only 7% of cases.[14]

Deborah's parents knew that she was not attending school but were unable to make or persuade her to go. She was a quiet girl who had been successful at primary school. Soon after transferring to the local comprehensive school she was taken ill, at school, with suspected appendicitis. Doctors could find no serious physiological cause for the pain and after a few days she was told that she could return to school. This led to an hysterical outburst. It emerged that Deborah had been bullied in the playground by a group of older girls, who had called her names, trampled on her bag and torn some of her books. This had made her late for a lesson, where she had been ridiculed by the teacher for being late, having damaged books and appearing dishevelled. She had been too afraid to tell the teacher about the incident in the playground. Her anxiety was so great that it was expressed, initially, through severe physical pain and subsequent refusal to attend school.

Bullying can make pupils anxious about attending school and can lead to unauthorised truancy.

Children may be afraid to tell teachers that they are being bullied.

Parents may know that their child is not attending school but feel unable to do anything about it.

11

In cases of extreme anxiety regarding school, children may be unable to attend for long periods of time. Additional help and support will be required in such cases from educational psychology or psychiatric services. Estimates of the numbers of children exhibiting extreme emotional responses to school vary from 0.4% to 1.7% of school-aged children.[15]

A number of common anxiety triggers are listed opposite. Some may be more relevant at primary than secondary level and vice versa, although many are common to both. Some may seem trivial but the effect on children should not be underestimated.

Children's anxieties and fears are not always as strong or obvious as those given in the case studies, but nevertheless are powerful enough to make some children want to avoid school some of the time. For pupils who are anxious absenteeism can provide a means of reducing anxiety but it can then create another anxiety, worry about being caught.

Holidays, special occasions, outside activities

Parents have the right to withdraw their children from school to participate in a day set aside exclusively for religious observance in the family faith. Schools can at their discretion also give permission for students to be absent. Whether the school chooses to do so depends on value judgements made about the particular activity. If the values of the pupils, parents and school differ and absence is not authorised this could precipitate future unauthorised absence. Schools may have to reach decisions regarding a variety of activities, for instance:

a two week holiday with parents

an extended visit of three months to visit relatives

attendance at a grandparent's birthday celebrations

attendance and participation in a regional skateboarding competition

representing a region in a national or international competition (sports, music, chess, etc)

attendance at a pop concert

What may create anxiety in pupils?

Anxiety about relationships

❏ aspects of teacher behaviour
❏ difficult relationships with teachers
❏ public criticism or ridicule
❏ difficulties in relationships with other children
❏ coping with being bullied
❏ coping with sexual harassment
❏ coping with racial harassment

Anxiety about academic performance

❏ a highly competitive atmosphere
❏ examination stress
❏ high levels of homework
❏ non-completion of homework
❏ inappropriate level of work (often too difficult but sometimes too easy)
❏ worry about failure

Anxiety about the environment

❏ lack of a positive working environment in class
❏ frequent changes of location
❏ the possibility of getting lost or being late for lessons
❏ inadequate toilet facilities (no locks on the door, dirty, smelly)
❏ embarrassment in changing for PE and taking communal showers

Family circumstances

Parental attitudes and influence

Although family circumstances can contribute towards absenteeism, families can also contribute to its reduction. A recent study[16] found that 44% of truants believed that their parents knew that they were truanting. However, 48% did not truant because they were afraid of their parents finding out. Even when parents are aware of a child's unauthorised absence they may not actively condone it. They may simply feel that enforcing their child's attendance at school is beyond their power. This can apply even when parents are faced with court appearances.

Helping at home

Children may be prevented from attending school by family demands on their time. Children can be deliberately kept away from school or may choose not to go. Some of the common reasons are:

helping to look after younger children

helping with housework

working in the family business

looking after a relative who is ill (this may be long or short-term)

providing company for a parent

waiting for the plumber, gasman, etc in the absence of parents

Extreme family pressures

Some children experience extremely difficult home circumstances. Coping with severe family stress may place such demands on the child that school is seen as relatively unimportant in their lives. Even for children where stress is not severe there may be a conflict of interests between a perceived need to be at home and the desire to go to school. Schools also have an important role in providing a stable, caring and supportive environment which may assist in coping with family difficulties. For some children home life may include:

alcoholism

drug abuse

sexual abuse

violence

unstable relationships between adults

difficult relationships between adults and children

an uncaring environment

unemployment

severe financial difficulties

illness

psychiatric disorder

lack of a proper home

If these factors do not prevent children from attending school they may affect their behaviour and performance. Some may understandably be present in body but absent in mind, while others may find school a place to release their own pent-up frustration and anger.

Families do not exist in isolation. They are part of a wider community within society. If that community is characterised by high unemployment and alienation from society this will inevitably affect children's attitudes. Schools cannot be expected to shoulder the responsibility for remedying such social problems alone.

Paul is nine. His mother suffers from periods of alcoholism. His father has recently left home after years of abusive and violent behaviour towards Paul, his younger sister, and their mother. Paul likes school, enjoys the company of other children, tries hard with his work and is progressing steadily. However he is often away from school because he is afraid to leave his mother and sister at home alone. He worries that his mother may have an accident during a drinking spell, may set fire to the house by leaving a cigarette alight or that his father may return and the violence recommence. For the same reason he is often afraid to go to sleep at night.

Children may feel that their fears and responsibilities at home are more pressing than their schooling.

Schools, possibly collaborating with other services, can provide stability and support in such cases.

15

Anne lives in an isolated spot in the countryside. Transport is difficult with few buses, which are some distance away. Often in the winter when the weather is bad the buses are cancelled. Anne's father cannot take her to school because he starts work early in the morning and his place of work is in the opposite direction to the school. There are no other families with children nearby who can offer help with transport. Mother stays at home looking after the younger children, while father works long hours. Since leaving primary school Anne has regularly taken time off school. She helps her mother look after the house and the younger children. When her mother is ill or has to go out she takes sole responsibility.

Problems with transport to school can set a pattern for absenteeism.

Parents may come to rely on help at home from their children.

Children may come to accept that education is not for them.

Issues within school

There are aspects of school life which, while they may not induce severe anxiety in the majority of students, may contribute towards apathy and alienation.

The school environment

Schools are often, through no fault of the staff, unattractive environmentally. Buildings may be dilapidated. Peeling paint, poor toilet facilities, lack of appropriate safe places for leaving belongings, and poor heating and ventilation are unlikely to encourage school attendance. Playgrounds can be drab and schools often lack alternative indoor accommodation, requiring pupils to go outside unless the weather is extremely severe. The opportunities for bullying also increase during these periods, when supervision is often left to untrained supervisors. Walking long distances between split sites also provides opportunities for skipping lessons.

School requirements

Some children are prevented or discouraged from attending school because of overstretched family finances. Difficulties in providing school uniform, appropriate shoes, PE kit, materials for design and technology can all contribute towards non-attendance. The cost of transport or deficiencies in its provision can also be important factors.

School circumstances

Circumstances within a school at particular times may also exacerbate non-attendance. Staff illness, frequent staff changes, restructuring, financial cutbacks, uncertainty regarding permanent school closure, temporary closures because of bad weather or school maintenance problems can all contribute to a lowering of morale and poor attendance.

In an upper school, taking students from year 9 onwards, it was noted from computerised attendance records that a particular year group had markedly poor overall attendance. Analysis of the reasons for this indicated that it was a 'difficult' year group. Also at their point of entry to the school a combination of circumstances including maternity leave, staff illness and secondment had led to several changes of head of year. This meant that the problem had not been identified and tackled early on.

Unauthorised absenteeism can arise from combinations of unforeseen circumstances in school.

Attitudes to school

Some children experience difficulties with the curriculum itself. Sometimes, this may manifest itself in 'absences of mind', ie children not paying attention. In combination with other factors it can lead to the skipping of particular lessons or even whole days of schooling. School work may be perceived as too difficult or irrelevant to such an extent that a child may feel that there is little point in attending school. Some young people feel they have no future. While they want a good job and feel qualifications would help they believe that these are out of their reach.

Despite this it seems that the majority of truants are not hostile to the process of education and many (60%) want to continue their education.[16] Two thirds do not dislike school or think it 'mostly enjoyable'. They merely express the desire to get out of particular classes from time to time. Reasons given for skipping individual lessons are given below.

	Student's response
The teacher is unpleasant	27%
The lesson is irrelevant	20%
The lesson is not enjoyable	14%
The lesson is too difficult	9%
Homework or coursework have not been completed	8%
The teacher is unhelpful	2%
The teacher is not interested	1%

Derived from *Truancy in English Secondary Schools: A Report for the DFE* by the Truancy Research Project, 1991-1992, University of North London Truancy Unit (1994) London: HMSO.

When individual subjects are considered, the percentage reporting truanting from PE is particularly high (34%). While some may perceive this as trivial, successfully skipping individual lessons can lead to more persistent absenteeism.[17,18]

For some persistent absentees school may be perceived as an alienating place, representative of the wider society from which they have also become alienated. Pupils may also reject the ethos and values of the school itself. The institutional aspects of schools, which require at least some degree of conformity, can provide a prime focus for rebellious and challenging behaviour in all students. This may centre on rules regarding dress or general appearance, required behaviour within the classroom, more general behaviour within the school environment or simply having to attend. It also seems that for pupils in some schools entering the world of work, either through work experience or part-time employment, may accentuate this process, making many school rules seem petty. Similarly, pupils who have family responsibilities to shoulder may resent their lack of autonomy within the school setting.

Teaching methods which deny pupils the opportunity to be independent in their learning may cause similar resentment, particularly in the later stages of schooling, and may contribute towards disruptive behaviour in the classroom. While minor disruptions in classrooms are part of the fabric of school life, in a minority of extreme cases pupils may severely disrupt lessons and become involved in serious incidents outside the classroom. When these pupils truant from school the remaining pupils and the teachers may welcome the opportunity to work in a relatively stress-free environment. This is understandable. However, passively ignoring the problems of disaffected students in this way solves nothing and denies those pupils the education to which they are entitled.

Attractions outside school

There is a popular misconception that children truant from school because the activities they undertake outside are more fun or interesting. As the previous sections illustrate the reasons for non-attendance are many and varied and are not often dependent on the attraction of competing activities.

When children themselves make an active decision to truant they often undertake activities with friends, although this is not necessarily the result of peer pressure. Students missing individual lessons often do not leave

Hazel is a high flier academically and expects to do well in her GCSEs, continue at school with 'A' levels and then go to university to study languages. Despite her positive overall attitude to education she loathes PE and finds it irrelevant to her needs. For exercise she prefers to go swimming and play badminton at the local leisure centre, where she does not have to endure the embarrassment of communal showers with other students. This has led to a fairly consistent skipping of PE lessons over the last year. On these occasions she does not leave the school but finds a quiet corner to get on with her studying.

Some pupils are not alienated from school as a whole but dislike particular lessons or teachers.

the school premises but find an isolated spot to smoke and talk, often the toilets. When taking a day off from school they may spend the time sleeping, watching videos with friends, having meals at each others houses or visiting the town. Some pupils become so alienated from the school environment that they drop out completely, becoming members of older friendship groups with more adult interests and concerns.

For some pupils, playing truant may initially create excitement. The fear of being caught and the sense of rebellion may provide heightened stimulation. If continued however, such sensations will dissipate and truancy can become routine, the norm.

There is currently concern regarding the employment of school-aged children. In the region of one million are employed illegally.[19] The attractions of work may be many: an improved financial position, the possibility of making a positive contribution to the family, responsibility, adult status, etc. Undertaking paid employment may contribute to truancy directly when the child skips school to go to work, and indirectly when the child may miss school because of tiredness, uncompleted homework or coursework. Research by North Tyneside council[20] shows a relationship between long hours spent working, low grades, low attendance rates and a weak commitment to continuing education. One in five of the 281 year 11 pupils interviewed were working in excess of ten hours a week.

Sue is 14 and prefers not to go to school. She can give no specific reason for this except to describe it as 'boring'. She prefers to spend her time at home, sleeping, or watching videos or TV. Sometimes she goes into the town with her friends, looking round the shops and meeting older boyfriends. Sometimes she helps her parents in their business. Her parents know that she skips school but are not unduly concerned. They left school at 16 themselves with no qualifications. Despite this they now run a thriving business and can see little point in Sue continuing at school. They have been taken to court in relation to her non-attendance and after this she did return to school for a while. But she soon slipped back into the previous pattern.

If the perceived rewards of going to school are not great pupils may see little point in attending, particularly if parents condone their absence.

What schools can do

No skipping allowe...

Truancy is now a political football. But, as
Reva Klein asks, what are the goals?

-tech scheme

stop truancy

...ard lines: the causes of truancy need to be better understood if the current calls for a clampdown are to be fair to chi...

...seem to be the almost uni-
...y despised subjects of PE
...rench and, to a lesser extent,
...ious education, science and

...social workers move towards pr
...venting the problem.
In 1991 city head teachers set t
Through the Net project to lo
...w. This project has carri
...into the problem.
...ember of t
...ho h

...uancy, not to be confused with
...bool refusal, where the child
...ys off school for long periods
...th the parents knowledge.
...iven that most students will take
...ne off occasionally and that a
...all, hard core will do it persis-
...ntly, is there anything that
...achers can do?
Dr John Pearce, professor of
...ild and adolescent psychiatry at
...ottingham University, believe
...is important for teachers
...derstand why children tru
...d what truancy can mea
...cir future. "There are the
...edisposing factors for pers
...ants as for delinquents.
...ildren tend to come fro
...nctional, disrupted
...y are often children
...ademically and
...often b

What schools can do

"create a warm, welcoming and secure atmosphere where children feel valued; provide a stimulating and accessible curriculum delivered in a physically clean, bright and attractive environment"

Aim from the attendance policy of Bayswater Middle School, Oxford

Most children have no choice but to attend school. It is for schools to make the experience a valuable one. To ensure full attendance and high motivation a school needs clear aims for pupils and high expectations of them. A climate needs to be created which allows for diversity, and provides high standards of education, protection and safety for all.

What steps can schools take to create such a climate? The following sections of this booklet offer practical ideas about how to improve attendance and promote a positive atmosphere within school. All of the items suggested have had successful outcomes in some schools. However, each school needs to establish those practices which are most appropriate for its needs. For this reason it is not possible to supply a single solution. Ideas will be presented, some of which may be helpful in your school.

Five key areas are considered. These demonstrate a progression through which appropriate practice and policy can be developed within an individual school:

❏ assessing the pattern of attendance

❏ promoting a positive school environment

❏ the daily management of attendance

❏ improving liaison outside school

❏ developing, communicating and evaluating policy

Assessing the pattern of attendance

Identifying patterns and causes of absence

Each school has its own characteristic pattern of attendance which is dependent on the nature of the school community and the school itself. To improve attendance schools must understand their existing pattern of attendance and the reasons for it.

Schools can take a number of steps to assist in this process:

analyse the data from school registers

monitor attendance at all lessons

monitor patterns of lateness

identify individuals and groups with poor attendance

identify particular lessons where students are truanting

identify possible reasons for poor attendance, overall and in particular lessons

A number of practical ways of establishing the reasons for non-attendance are:

giving questionnaires to pupils

having discussions or brainstorming sessions about the reasons for non-attendance in pupil tutorials

initiating teacher groups to discuss their worries and problems and how things might be improved

setting up meetings with members of outside agencies, eg EWOs, social workers, who have access to other perspectives on the school

setting up meetings of parents to discuss attendance issues

sending letters of enquiry to parents regarding school attendance with slips for them to respond

using teacher researchers taking higher degrees, seconded through GEST projects, or undertaking inservice training to assist in establishing attendance patterns and the underlying reasons for them

The information derived from these enquiries can be used to identify:

the baseline attendance rates for classes, year groups and the whole school

the particular types of absence prevalent in the school

lessons where truancy occurs

pupils or groups of pupils whose absence gives cause for concern

connections between school events and reduced attendance, eg staff training days, mock examinations, absence of form tutor

possible reasons for absence

areas where action needs to be taken

If schools are anxious to make immediate changes to promote attendance, the assessment procedure may seem tedious and time-consuming. But this stage is necessary to avoid implementing inappropriate policies and procedures.

The monitoring of absence may reveal particular groups of children with attendance problems. These may relate to gender, ethnic groupings, where they live, their home circumstances or difficulties with the curriculum.

Schools can also adopt strategies to identify those aspects of school which might be improved to actively promote attendance. For instance, brainstorming sessions can help to identify what staff and students believe to be the characteristics of a good school. This can provide a framework for future planning. An example of the outcome of such a session is given on page 26.

Raising awareness

Attendance is the responsibility of all staff, parents, pupils and governors. For sustained improvement, the impetus for change should be shared by everyone concerned. Attendance issues need to be given a high profile. Pupils and parents need to be persuaded of the benefits of being in school. Members of the local community can also be encouraged to take an interest.

The importance of attendance at school can be raised in various ways. Schools have:

used theatre-in-education groups

instigated poster competitions

taken part in local carnivals with floats promoting attendance at school

provided attendance notice boards giving details of current attendance figures

sent leaflets to parents

used the local press

stressed the dangers for truants

persuaded local shops and services to provide goods as incentives for good attendance

persuaded local industry to provide work experience placements for persistent absentees, dependent on good school attendance

raised their profile by playing a useful part in the community

Characteristics of a good school

A feeling of community
- ❏ Good relationships
- ❏ Happy people
- ❏ Not being afraid
- ❏ Students not picked on by staff - No bullying
- ❏ Talking openly and honestly

A positive atmosphere
- ❏ Lots of praise for achievement, academic and non-academic
- ❏ Everyone making progress
- ❏ Exciting, not boring
- ❏ Relevant, interesting

A broad view of education
- ❏ Being concerned with more than the National Curriculum
- ❏ Continuing education
- ❏ Contact after leaving school
- ❏ Extra curricular activities

An attractive environment
- ❏ Respect for the environment and buildings

A sense of purpose
- ❏ People should be punctual
- ❏ The school should be efficient

A self-critical stance
- ❏ Openness to change
- ❏ Be self-critical

Peers School, Oxford

Summary

Assessing the pattern of attendance

❏ Attendance is the responsibility of all staff, parents, pupils and governors.

❏ Each school needs to study its own characteristic pattern of absence.

❏ This can be established by monitoring half day and lesson attendance.

❏ Groups and individuals with persistent attendance problems can be identified.

❏ Through consultation, the reasons for unauthorised absence can be established.

❏ Action plans can be developed to promote attendance.

Promoting a positive school environment

This section will consider issues relating to the school climate and facilities, teacher/pupil relationships, classroom practices, the curriculum, the physical environment and staff training.

The school climate and facilities

The social climate of the school is critical in creating a suitable environment for learning. If children are afraid of being bullied and there is disruption both in and out of lessons, the possibility of effective learning taking place will be considerably reduced. Alternatively, if there is mutual respect, clear communication and well-focused attention to a wide range of achievement, the possibilities will be great.

To promote positive patterns of behaviour and attendance, schools may find it useful to develop a code of behaviour and outline the rights and responsibilities of pupils and staff. An example of a bill of rights is given opposite.

Once the code of behaviour has been established, through consultation with staff, pupils and parents, its impact needs to be sustained. This will be assisted by:

staff at all levels consistently referring to it

firm and fair action being taken where there is evidence of inappropriate behaviour in pupils or staff

the positive aspects of the behaviour and work of staff and pupils being emphasised, praised and rewarded

the setting up of school councils or other mechanisms to allow pupils to influence decision-making

providing systems where pupils know help and advice is available, eg counselling services, tutorial support

regular discussion and review of the code of behaviour

While teachers and the adult world in general perceive the purpose of attending school in educational terms, pupils often see it as a place to meet friends and have fun. Where children have developed friendships and an enjoyable social life they are likely to attend school regularly. If bullying is rife the social aspects of schooling can become intolerable for some children.

Brownhills High School Bill of Rights

Rights and Responsibilities

1 We have the right not to be bullied in any way, shape or form.

   We have the responsibility not to bully others and to report any bullying we see.

2 We have the right to feel safe in and around the school.

   We have the responsibility to ensure the safety of all pupils by behaving in a reasonable manner in and around school.

3 We have the right to an education and to learn according to our ability.

   We have the responsibility not to ridicule others for the way in which they learn, or to disturb the learning of others.

4 We have the right to be treated with respect by all people irrespective of age, gender, colour or status.

   We have the responsibility to respect all others within our community.

5 We have the right to express our own opinions and to be heard.

   We have the responsibility to allow others to express their opinions and to be heard.

6 We have the right to expect that our possessions will be secure in and around school.

   We have the responsibility not to steal or mistreat the possessions of others and to report any theft or mistreatment that we see.

7 We have the right to choose our friends.

   We have the responsibility not to force our friendship upon others or to abuse the friendship.

8 We have the right to play in safety and without interference.

   We have the responsibility not to disrupt, or endanger, the play of others.

At primary level potential non-attenders are supported by personal relationships, which can flourish in smaller institutions where there are fewer adults, smaller buildings and a comfortable, safe environment. It is significant that students often visit their primary school even when they have moved on to secondary education. Secondary schools can promote such an environment by:

   accepting that older students need time and space for themselves and make this possible

   ensuring that playgrounds are safe environments, eg by staggering lunch-times and providing training for ancillary staff

   providing access to sports facilities, the library, and social areas during break times

   encouraging students to become involved in and initiate after-school and lunch-time activities, social occasions, homework clubs, etc

   making arrangements for the school to provide breakfast

   paying attention to the quality of personal relationships throughout the school

   ensuring a high quality of personal-social education to facilitate the understanding of personal relationships

Teacher/pupil relationships

Teacher/pupil relationships are central within school.

Although not all pupils and teachers can relate easily to one another there need to be minimum standards of behaviour on both sides. The development of a code of behaviour, which stresses the importance of mutual respect will assist in this process. The school needs to have clear expectations of staff and pupils and to demonstrate consistency in challenging breaches of the code.

The evidence reported earlier[21] indicates that dislike of particular teachers is the major cause of post-registration truancy. What pupils dislike are teachers who are 'unpleasant'. Teachers need to treat pupils with respect, whatever their personal feelings towards them.

What can schools do to ensure that this is the case? Support systems can be established within the school providing advice and assistance for teachers experiencing difficult classroom situations. A clear system of referral for pupils who are causing problems may also be helpful.

Appraisal can provide an appropriate forum to raise such issues with teachers. Training may then be indicated, eg in interpersonal skills, dealing with difficult behaviour. Sources of information regarding training are given at the end of this booklet.

Classroom practices

Successful classroom practices are those which encourage students to become involved with their work. Motivating pupils is one of the most important tasks of a teacher. How can teachers improve student motivation? While it is beyond the scope of this booklet to cover these issues in depth the box on the following page provides a framework which might be adapted to suit the needs of particular schools. Sources for further reading are given at the end of the booklet.

Supporting learning within the curriculum

Some pupils 'bunk off' because they dislike particular lessons. The percentage reported in recent research[24] for different subjects is given below.

PE/Games	34%
French	27%
RE	20%
Maths	19%
Science	19%
History	19%
English	18%
Technology	16%
Geography	16%

Despite the changes recommended in the Dearing report[25] the National Curriculum exerts considerable constraints on the freedom of schools to develop their own curriculum. However, schools do have control over the way in which the curriculum is delivered. It may be that preferences for different lessons are a reflection of the way that they are taught. A simple questionnaire to pupils can establish the pattern of lesson preferences in individual schools. This can provide the basis for implementing necessary change.

Engaging classrooms

Derived from the work of Ames (1992)[22] and Epstein (1989)[23]

In what ways can classrooms encourage a positive style of learning motivation?

Tasks

❏ design activities that make learning interesting and that involve variety and personal challenge

❏ help learners establish realistic goals. With short-term goals, students view their classwork as manageable, and they can focus on their progress and what they are learning

❏ help students develop organisational and management skills and effective task strategies. Students, especially those with learning difficulties, need to develop and apply strategies for planning, organising and monitoring their work

Authority

❏ give students opportunities to participate actively in the learning process via leadership roles, choices and decision-making

❏ help students develop the skills that will enable them to take responsibility for their learning

Recognition

❏ recognise individual student effort, accomplishments and improvement

❏ give all students opportunities to receive reward and recognition

❏ give recognition and rewards privately so that their value is not derived at the expense of others

Grouping

❏ provide opportunities for co-operative group learning and peer interaction

❏ use heterogeneous and varied grouping arrangements

Evaluation

❏ evaluate students for individual progress, improvement and mastery

❏ give students opportunities to improve their performance

❏ vary the method of evaluation and make evaluation private

Time

❏ adjust task or time requirements for students who have difficulty completing their work

❏ allow students opportunities to plan their schedules and progress at an optimal rate

All pupils may experience difficulties related to the curriculum at some time during their years at school. This may lead to a reluctance to attend certain lessons. Provision of specific support and guidance from the school may prevent this. Help can be given in relation to:

catching up with work when pupils have been absent for any reason

keeping up with work through a long absence, eg providing distance learning materials

anxiety regarding examinations

time management and study skills

making appropriate option choices for year 10

Some pupils are particularly vulnerable with respect to the curriculum. For instance, there is a strong link between poor attendance and poor literacy. Children whose first language is not English may also be at risk. Where schools have provided special voluntary classes for improving literacy, these have proved popular with pupils, literacy has improved and there has been a subsequent improvement in attendance. Such intervention is likely to be more successful if undertaken early in a pupil's school career.

Some schools provide support teachers and assistants to help pupils with learning difficulties in curriculum lessons. This can be a particularly effective way of ensuring access to the curriculum. Through the personal attention and encouragement offered by the assistant, pupils' motivation to learn can improve. Motivation can also be sustained by the provision of tasks appropriate to the pupils' needs. The differentiation of the curriculum is a key factor in helping pupils engage with learning tasks and achieve appropriate National Curriculum levels.

Exam entry policies are also important. Those students who are not entered may see little point in attending school. To raise achievement, schools may wish to enter as many pupils as possible for GCSE. Where GCSE entry has been seen as inappropriate for particular pupils, some schools have explored alternatives. A small range of vocational qualifications are becoming available and some schools have provided opportunities for students to take basic skills tests in numeracy and literacy. These have improved motivation and attendance.

Many schools provide opportunities for work experience for all their pupils. For persistent truants, carefully monitored work placements can be incorporated into an individual education plan, with a full time-table consisting of school and work. Where links with local companies have been developed and the company provides a mentor, these have proved extremely successful and persistent absentees can be achieving 100% attendance within a few weeks, eg COMPACT PLUS or STEP (School Time Enterprise Programme) schemes. Some schools have developed opportunities for pupils to undertake work related activities within the school, eg developing small business or practical projects.

The physical environment

Making major changes to the physical environment of the school can be constrained by financial considerations. However, smaller projects are often possible with the assistance of the local community, parental efforts and links with local industry. Such projects have the added advantage of increasing feelings of ownership and commitment to the school.

While schools have a responsibility to satisfy health and safety requirements, further enhancement of the physical fabric of the school will be at the school's discretion. Some important aspects of the physical environment that might be considered are:

general cleanliness, litter, graffiti

heating and lighting

decoration, pictures, displays of work

safe storage for pupils' belongings

safe social areas for each year group

notice boards in tutorial rooms to be the responsibility of the pupils

a quiet study room

an indoor games room

clean and appropriate toilet facilities

a welcoming entrance hall with a clearly signposted reception area for visitors

a pleasantly decorated parents' room

Implications for staff training

In attempting to create a positive school climate schools may find that staff require additional training.

Teaching staff may benefit from training related to:

anti-bullying procedures

dealing with disruptive behaviour

classroom management
interpersonal skills
teaching using the media
differentiation
teaching basic skills

Within school, opportunities can also be created for teachers to observe each other at work to develop new ideas and provide examples of good practice.

Ancillary staff may benefit from training relating to bullying in the playground and maintaining positive behaviour at lunch-time.

Further information regarding training is provided at the end of the booklet.

Summary

Promoting a positive school environment

A positive social climate is created when:

- ❏ there is a code of conduct for pupils and staff
- ❏ good behaviour is praised
- ❏ student participation in decision-making is encouraged
- ❏ lessons are interesting
- ❏ there is constructive feedback
- ❏ autonomous, independent learning is encouraged
- ❏ the curriculum is relevant and interesting
- ❏ help with basic skills is provided
- ❏ the physical environment is safe and pleasant
- ❏ appropriate training opportunities are provided

The daily management of attendance

Monitoring attendance

Half day attendance

If schools are to improve attendance they must have accurate and systematic ways of recording it. Schools need to identify their attendance pattern and their starting point for improving attendance. There are also legal requirements relating to recording attendance which schools must satisfy (see appendix).

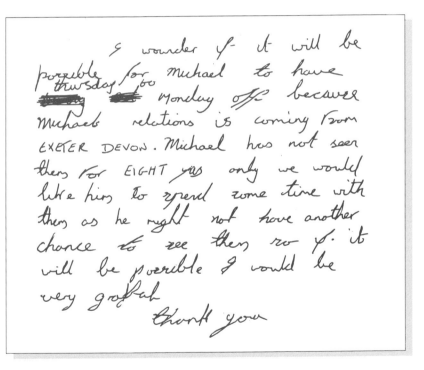

In monitoring the pattern of attendance, some schools have found it necessary to:

redesign school registers to allow for more data to be recorded

develop coding systems to record more detailed information

devise ways of recording lateness

devise ways of presenting data so that it is easy to understand

revise procedures for the collection of registers

ensure that all registers are completed in the same way

use computers for recording information

provide pupils with passes for occasions when they have permission to be out of school

change the timing of work experience or staff days to lessen disruption to attendance patterns

Computer systems for recording attendance can:

provide accurate information

organise and analyse data quickly

provide long-term statistics to assist with the planning and analysis of patterns of absence

free staff time for follow up of non-attendance

They **cannot**, on their own, improve attendance at school.

If computer systems are installed staff will need training in their use. The school also needs to devise contingency plans should the computer system malfunction.

Lesson attendance

Traditional procedures for monitoring attendance at lessons may be adopted:

taking a register for every lesson

having random checks on lesson attendance (fairly frequently)

monitoring particular students who are known to 'bunk off'

patrolling school premises, particularly toilets and other places where pupils are known to meet

Some schools have installed computer systems for monitoring attendance at every lesson. This often involves teachers filling in an optical mark reader, although some systems work on swipe cards.

Those schools where monitoring attendance at individual lessons has been computerised have pointed out the following advantages and disadvantages:

❑ Every pupil is tracked throughout each day clearly indicating if a lesson is missed.

❑ Subject teachers become involved in the monitoring of attendance.

❑ Feedback is quick with a fast response to absence.

❑ Daily patterns of attendance can be studied.

❑ Attendance at particular lessons can be monitored.

❑ Timetabling problems can be identified.

❑ Attendance moves from a pastoral to a whole school responsibility.

❑ Form tutors see the information as useful.

❑ Pupils realise that they can no longer avoid detection.

❑ Attendance at lessons improves.

However,

❑ Setting up computer systems is a complex, time-consuming task.

❑ Issues surrounding accountability need to be handled with care.

> Steven was absent from School Friday because my daughter was rushed into hospital on Thursday night we didn't get home until the early hours.
> At the moment we are in utter chaos with having to go back and forth to the hospital
> Hope you understand
> yours Sincerely

Follow up needs

Whatever system of monitoring attendance is used it must meet the needs of those following up absence. Staff working on a daily basis in such a capacity are often able to feed back useful improvements on the basis of their experiences. This may relate to the ways that attendance information is recorded or the means by which unauthorised absence is followed up.

Procedures for when a child is absent from school

Parental response

Parents or carers can inform schools of a child's absence by personal contact, a note or letter, or a telephone call. If telephone calls are to become the normal procedure schools might consider having additional phone lines installed so that parents are not constantly faced with an engaged line which can be discouraging.

The school needs to consider whether a child's absence will automatically be designated as authorised if a note or telephone call is received from home. If not, under what circumstances will they be queried? In particular cases, where there is reason to doubt the authenticity of notes received from parents, the school may wish to keep records of the parents' signatures.

School response

To be effective a school's follow up to unauthorised absence needs to be speedy and consistent.

Speed of response to non-attendance

A prompt response by schools to unauthorised absence has the effect of reducing the length and frequency of absences.

Contact can be made by letter or telephone. A friendly response on the first day of absence is very effective. Personalised letters have a greater effect than standard letters. Telephone calls have the advantage that they cannot be intercepted by pupils. Where families do not have a telephone they are usually able to provide the number of a relative, friend or neighbour where they can be contacted. In some circumstances home visits may be needed. They are often much appreciated by families and can be very effective. However, there may be practical difficulties and they require more investment of time.

Consistency of response

To be effective the response from the school must be consistent, thorough and well publicised. The follow up must be carried out in the same way for each pupil on every occasion of absence. Many schools have found it useful to draw up a flow chart which demonstrates their procedures for following up absence. This is likely to include phone calls, letters, home visits and invitations for the parents to visit the school. A possible framework for considering such procedures is provided on page 42.

Some schools have devised a series of phased letters, which are sent out at various stages in a long period of absence. The letters set out points in the procedure, invite parents to the school to discuss issues, and remind parents of their legal responsibilities and the possible penalties for non-attendance. Parents are informed when the case will be referred to EWOs.

During a long absence schools may wish to remain in contact with the pupil directly, whether the absence is authorised or not. This may be undertaken on a weekly basis, by telephoning to see how they are, sending a card from the class, sending a class newsletter, encouraging visits from class members or visits from teachers. Schools are also expected to set work for long-term absentees, for instance those who are ill or afraid to attend school, and to co-operate with home tuition services. Such procedures will help the pupil to feel that they have a place in the school and may help in the process of returning to school when it occurs.

Follow up of absence

1 Child is absent.

2 Record absence.

3 If the parents have not already contacted the school seek an explanation for absence as soon as possible, preferably on the first day.

4 If a satisfactory explanation is given record absence as authorised.

5 If the child is going to be legitimately absent for a long period of time ensure that the school provides work and maintains contact.

6 If no satisfactory explanation for the absence is given record the absence as unauthorised and make contact with the parents to discuss the problem.

7 If this is unsuccessful in resolving the problem consult with other relevant agencies, eg EWOs, Educational Psychologists.

Lateness

Systems to monitor school attendance should also take account of lateness. Specific codes should indicate in the register when a child is late. After a period of 30 minutes has lapsed the child is normally counted as an unauthorised absentee for that half day. Procedures should be set down clearly and pupils and parents should be made aware of them. They should also be used consistently across the school. A combination of reward and punishment is likely to be most effective for combating lateness (see page 44).

Staffing

Whatever procedures are set up for the monitoring and follow up of unauthorised absence a decision will have to be made about who is to be responsible for the follow up. For some tasks it may be most appropriate and cost effective to employ ancillary staff:

    to operate computer systems

    carry out clerical and administrative work associated with monitoring and recording attendance

However, responsibility for the long-term monitoring and follow up of individual absence will need to be taken by a member or members of the teaching staff. This may be the form tutor, the head of year, the deputy head or combinations of these.

Effective practice in relation to the individual pupil usually involves the form tutor. This enables close relationships to develop. If form tutors are to follow up absence and take responsibility for attendance in their form they need:

    time

    support

    to feel that the work is valued

    training in making effective use of their time

    training in the skills of individual tutoring

> I'm sorry Tania was absent yesterday but I'm poorly with flu and I needed her at home. Also last Friday she was away because she had a bad headache
>
> Yours Sincerely

Practices which have proved effective in supporting tutors include:

co-ordination and monitoring of the work of tutors by the head of year or team teacher to ensure consistency

cover being provided for some tutorial sessions to enable tutors to interview individual students

discussion of attendance issues, individual and group, at regular year meetings

liaison with EWOs and year tutors to plan strategies for individual pupils with attendance problems

provision of time for tutors to deal with tutorial work

organisation of regular meetings between academic and pastoral networks to communicate information regarding post-registration truancy

Rewarding good attendance and punctuality

A reward system for good attendance and punctuality can improve both. The best systems are cumulative, initially providing rewards for short periods of time, eg two weeks, with increases up to a term and then a year. This gradual build up of rewards promotes self-monitoring. Such rewards are particularly effective when they are part of the school's general system of rewards for achievement. The link is then made between good attendance and success in school. Pupil diaries are a useful way of keeping records of attendance, achievement, lateness and homework. Rewards can also be given to groups of pupils, classes, house groups and year groups.

Rewards favoured by students include stickers which can be placed in easily visible places, merit points, certificates to be included in National Records of Achievement, letters to parents, tuck shop tokens, personalised prizes which are visible in school, eg inscribed pens or key rings, tokens which can be exchanged for goods, school prizes. Each school should consult its pupils about the nature of the rewards to be given as this may vary. School trips, particularly those which involve overnight stays, are valued by pupils and also serve to strengthen group relationships.

For younger pupils competitions can be run between classes. These have proved to be successful and popular. One school used a mascot (a small bear) as a prize. This was awarded on a temporary basis until the next competition.

It is important as part of the reward system to give attendance issues a high profile, for instance, by using:

assemblies to reward and provide information about attendance

displays at parents' evenings

attendance notice boards, which display current information

Working with individuals

The attendance patterns of individual children may be identified as giving cause for concern. For these individuals the school will need to take specific action. This will include contact with parents and an attempt to ascertain the reason for the absenteeism.

The parents may be:

unaware of the absence

aware but unable or unwilling to do anything about it

actively encouraging the absence

On the basis of discussions with the child and his or her parents the school will need to devise an **action plan**. This will outline the steps the pupil can take, the support required to bring about change, and the time scale for action and review.

Problems within school

The problem may be located within the school. For instance:

as a result of poor relationships between the pupil and staff

as a response to bullying or poor peer relationships

as a response to anxiety regarding work

In these cases the school can directly implement the necessary plan and monitor its effectiveness. Expert advice should be sought at an early stage so that it is possible to establish the seriousness of the case and determine what action should be taken. Particular skills, eg counselling, may be required to support the child during this time. Often, the person best placed to help the child and his/her family is the one with whom the child has the best relationship. This may be a member of the teaching staff, a youth worker, an ancillary worker, a family member or other professional such as an education welfare officer. In these cases it is important that whoever carries out the day-to-day work of negotiation

45

and counselling is given appropriate professional support.

The circumstances of each case will be unique and require different combinations of strategies. Some suggestions for action with the pupil are given below:

social skills training

counselling with a trained counsellor

designating an individual member of staff as a mentor

developing a modified time-table

regularly reviewing progress

providing a support assistant to work with the individual in class and during social times

Problems outside school

If the problem is located elsewhere, in the family or as a result of other pressures, the school will need to make contact with other agencies, eg education welfare officers, social workers, educational psychologists, health service workers. Poor attenders are often disregarded as a group requiring special needs support and attention. Under the terms of the 1989 Children Act, such matters as childhood stress and poverty are regarded as expressions of need contributing towards under-achievement and disaffection at school.

> Would you please allow Natalie to come home after her dinner today. She has a couple of jobs I need doing in Oxford. As yet I'm not strong enough to go into Oxford. Natalie was absent last week with an ear infection and a cold
>
> Yours Sincerely

Some children may need professional help, eg from counsellors or educational psychologists, while for others a more disciplinarian approach may be adopted. Work may be undertaken with the whole family. In some cases, the LEA may feel it necessary to take parents to court. The school will be involved in this process to the extent that they will be required to provide relevant information about the child's attendance and a more general report on the child in relation to school. The school should provide support for the child at all stages in this process.

Returning to school after a period of absence

This can be an uncomfortable time for the child and for the rest of the class. Friendship groups may have altered and changes may have taken place for which both parties must be prepared.

A number of strategies may be adopted to help a child return to school after a long absence:

the active involvement of school staff in the planning process

a welcoming attitude from staff and the avoidance of sarcastic comments

a visit to the school by the pupil prior to return to overcome initial fears

part-time attendance or a reduced time-table to ease the pupil back into the routine

special teaching provision and help catching up on work

the provision of a mentor, with whom the pupil has a special relationship and time to report to him or her during the day

preparation of the class for the pupil's return

a 'welcome back' card from the class

role play of difficult situations prior to returning to school

counselling provision

rewards for achievement in school work

Group work

Some secondary schools have set up groups for poor attenders. The members of these groups can be regular absentees or those who are felt to be at risk. Effective improvement has been achieved with pupils at transfer from primary school and between years seven to nine. For an effective outcome the pupils must want to attend, they should be of a similar age and their parents should be supportive. Meetings usually take place weekly. They concentrate on attendance, behavioural problems, relationships with authority figures, learning difficulties, working together, group identity, friendship and confidence building. In almost all cases there is considerable improvement in attendance. Groups can be run by the head of year, the school counsellor, or other appropriately skilled members of staff.

Staff training

The implications for staff training are considerable.

Staff may need training in relation to:

    attendance regulations

    new registration or monitoring procedures

    analysing attendance data

    follow up procedures

    interpersonal communication skills

    reward systems

    procedures for returners

    counselling

    tutoring individuals

    working with groups

Summary

The daily management of attendance

The school:

❏ keeps appropriate attendance records

❏ monitors patterns of attendance

❏ monitors post-registration truancy

❏ is consistent about the implementation of whole school policy, building this into other systems, eg appraisal

❏ decides on the most effective use of staff to implement the system and provides appropriate resources for the task to be undertaken effectively

❏ follows up individual cases of unauthorised or prolonged absence

❏ establishes the reasons for absence on the basis of discussions with pupil and parents

❏ consults with other professionals as necessary

❏ draws up an action plan and review programme

❏ provides appropriate training of staff and maintains this regularly

Improving liaison outside school

Responsibilities of schools

Schools monitor student attendance and therefore have responsibility for making contact with other agencies should the need arise. It is helpful if school staff understand the structure of other agencies, their lines of communication, their function and their thresholds for accepting referrals. Schools can go beyond this and establish strong links with families, communities, other schools and outside agencies so that prevention rather than cure becomes the norm.

Links with families

Schools need to foster links with families. Attendance at school is a matter of joint concern for schools and parents. Where parents themselves have had negative experiences of school they may be reluctant to make contact, even at primary level. Where attendance is good, hard pressed teachers may not wish to invest time in developing close links with parents. However, good relationships with families can be of great benefit to pupils.

Links with parents can be improved in a number of ways. Some of these may be more appropriate to primary or secondary school but many apply to both:

easy access for parents to see teachers

a welcoming atmosphere especially at parents' evenings

inviting parents to make presentations or help in the classroom

making some examination classes available to adults

encouraging PTAs

encouraging the use of the school for community events

valuing parent governors

writing a newsletter for parents and seeking their views

making links with local family centres

An illustration of how a school in Southwark set up an informal parents' evening is given opposite.

Informal parents' evenings

Tables and chairs were set up in a café style in the school hall. There were displays of work, videos of children engaged in learning activities, an attendance display, flowers, refreshments and background music. An introductory talk was followed by informal discussion and musical entertainment was provided by the school choir. Letters and personal invitations were posted to parents' homes. Staff wore name tags, and their photographs were on display. Parents could take part in activities, work with computers, and fill in worksheets. A prize draw was held based on the return of the posted invitation. The evening was very successful.

Links with the community

Community groups, including religious bodies, Community Service Volunteers, youth groups, and local industry can promote attendance at school by emphasising the importance of education for young people, working closely with the school and providing opportunities for work experience. Close links with local industry can be particularly important for the development of COMPACT schemes, in which industry and schools work together for their mutual benefit. Such schemes can increase motivation and improve attendance at school among a large number of pupils. There are also local schemes aimed specifically at the disaffected and those at risk of exclusion, eg COMPACT PLUS, STEP. Here the pupil is offered an opportunity to visit a local business on a day release basis for one day a week for a year to learn what will be required of him or her in the job market. Continuation of the scheme depends on the young person agreeing to abide by the rules of the company and attending regularly at school. Such schemes have been extremely successful.

In some areas, police, local businesses and shopkeepers have been involved in joint 'Truancy Watch' schemes to improve school attendance. The evidence indicates that such schemes may be effective in the short-term.[26] Staff in participating businesses and shops are informed of school dates and times and told how to approach truants. Pupils require a pass to authorise legitimate absence which they can show if challenged. Such campaigns receive considerable publicity and are valuable in raising awareness regarding the importance of school attendance.

Links with other schools

Liaison between primary and secondary schools is particularly important. Patterns of absence established in the primary school may continue in the secondary school. Information regarding attendance may therefore be important for preventing absence. Links between parents and school at primary level also need to be continued on transfer.

How might such links be encouraged? Ideas are suggested below:

joint artistic or musical productions, eg concerts, plays

presentations given at primary schools by secondary subject specialists

primary visits to secondary schools for special projects

liaison on curricula matters

joint planning in relation to school transfer

work experience undertaken in other local schools

Links with Education Welfare Officers

Education Welfare Officers, employed by the LEA, have legal duties when individual pupils are persistently absent from school. Education Welfare Officers can help schools by:

carrying out random immediate response visits to pupils' homes when absence is unauthorised

assisting in support units or drop in services for pupils with attendance problems

setting up joint visits of EWOs and teachers to pupils' homes

liaising with social services

alerting schools to policies which may be causing disaffection, eg uniform, setting and banding arrangements

providing information about prosecution procedures

providing inservice training on a range of attendance related issues

Schools can enhance the benefit of their relationships with EWOs by:

frequent contact

frequent consultation regarding individual cases

acting upon feedback given in relation to school matters

ensuring that they are an integral part of the school and not a bolt-on extra

Other agencies

In severe cases of non-attendance multi-agency approaches are almost always required. This may require liaison with the police, health service workers, social workers, EWOs, youth workers, and educational psychologists. The children involved can be among the most complex of special needs cases. Child protection procedures or statements of special educational needs may need to be made. To minimise the disruption to a child's education it is essential that the school maintains liaison with a range of professionals and provides support for the child and his or her family.

In such cases there can be a tendency for children to 'fall through the cracks', in what have been described as 'circles of blame' where each agency or institution blames the other.[27] Schools can provide a centre for co-ordinating liaison between groups to attempt to ensure that the best interests of the child are served.

Regular meetings between representatives of differing agencies can provide opportunities to share concerns and to discuss issues arising from caseloads. Inter-agency meetings can also make it possible to explore and identify new groups which may be giving cause for concern, eg young carers, those with eating disorders or the recently bereaved.

How can schools improve liaison?

by convening regular meetings where all agencies can air and discuss common problems and possible solutions

by giving members of staff responsibility for liaison with particular agencies

by giving members of staff responsibility for particular children who are known to have extensive problems

Implications for training

In promoting links with the wider community and other agencies it is important that staff receive appropriate training and information. It would be helpful for them to have an understanding of:

the way that outside agencies operate

the make up of the community within which the school is located

the values of that community

the ethnic, religious, and cultural customs within the community

Summary

Improving liaison outside school

Schools:

❏ take the initiative in referring cases to other agencies

❏ promote links with parents

❏ promote links with the wider community and partner schools

❏ take full advantage of the services offered by EWOs

❏ are aware of the functioning of other agencies in cases where pupils have severe problems

❏ provide appropriate training opportunities for all their staff

Developing, communicating and evaluating policy

This booklet has described some of the ways that schools might improve attendance and establish procedures and practices appropriate for its daily monitoring and management. These, together, constitute the school's attendance policy. This should be formally documented and communicated to pupils, parents, and other members of the school community. Procedures also need to be established for review and evaluation of policy and practice.

Writing the policy document

The written policy should set down:

1 the aim of the school in relation to improving attendance

2 the ways that the school will actively encourage attendance by promoting a positive school environment

3 the reward system for good attendance

4 parental legal responsibilities in relation to school attendance. This should also include information on punctuality (see appendix)

5 the policy of the school for authorising absence from school in special circumstances, eg holidays, bereavement, competitions. The school needs to have agreed criteria for the kinds of circumstances which will be accepted, even if in practice there is some flexibility. These guidelines will need to be based on the needs of the community and the kinds of reasons they may have for wishing their children to take leave of absence. Consideration also needs to be given to the special needs of particular groups, eg children of travellers, religious faiths

6 how parents can apply for leave of absence for pupils

7 procedures by which parents should contact the school in case of absence

8 the procedures that the school will adopt in relation to the follow up of absence in the short and long-term

9 the procedures that the school will adopt for referral of cases to EWOs

10 the procedures for a child's return to school

The written document should take account of the DFEE guidelines for attendance (see appendix for resumé).

The school may also wish to consider the criteria set out for OFSTED inspections. Where attendance for classes or years falls below 90% inspectors will investigate the school's initiatives to improve matters. Punctuality will also be considered in relation to the start of the school day and individual lessons.

The evidence used by OFSTED will include:

registers of attendance, to confirm compliance with statutory requirements and allow for the assessment of any significant patterns of absence

attendance statistics for the school, to be compared with that from schools of similar characteristics nationally

observation of registration periods

attendance at and lateness for lessons

discussions with staff, the Education Welfare Officer and pupils, to establish the affects of attendance and punctuality on teaching, attainment and progress

the school's policy and any other documentation on attendance including sixth form attendance; and planned strategies to support individual pupils on their return from a period of extended absence

consultation with parents at the pre-inspection meeting.

Communication of policy

The policy needs to be communicated to parents and pupils. The school prospectus should include information on attendance, but further information might be communicated in newsletters, at parents' evenings, through PTAs, local community leaders, etc.

Schools might also consider:

translations of leaflets into languages used in the local community

the use of humour

the use of cartoons

the use of a tear-off slip on letters to parents to make it easier for them to make individual appointments

Communication needs to be repeated regularly for the families of pupils new to the school.

In addition to communicating parents' legal requirements regarding school attendance, schools may find it beneficial to publicise the signs of non-attendance. Many parents do not condone truancy and may be unaware that their child is truanting.

Signs of children not attending school

❏ sudden lack of homework
❏ a noticeable lack of interest in school
❏ no school communications
❏ an interest in where the parent will be during the day
❏ friends who are known truants
❏ a detailed knowledge of videos or daytime TV programmes
❏ attempts to keep parents away from school events
❏ a keenness to get to the post before parents (to intercept letters from school)

Derived from a leaflet produced by Hounslow Education Authority

Evaluating the effectiveness of policy and procedures

The information gathered through monitoring and review can be used to refine policy and practice increasing their effectiveness.

Opportunities for feedback on attendance levels, procedures and effective practices need to be created, for instance:

on an attendance notice board

at staff meetings

at governors' meetings

at school council meetings

at parents' evenings

in meetings with outside agencies

A policy document setting out the school's current practices relating to the improvement of attendance may provide a set of successful criteria. As such it can be revised annually and the policy becomes a living document. Some of these criteria constitute bench marks against which to measure improvements year by year as part of the school development plan. Examples are:

improved attendance

a decrease in the percentage of pupils not entered for any public examination reduced numbers of fixed term exclusions

an increase in the number of successful returns to full or part-time education by those excluded or truanting

an increase in staying-on rates post-sixteen

reduced incidents of harassment and bullying particularly in social times

space made available in agendas for policy making in relation to attendance and motivation

an increase in staff development in relation to the promotion of good attendance

an increase in parent and student satisfaction

Summary

Developing, communicating and evaluating policy

The policy:

❏ embodies the school's aims and practices to improve attendance

❏ outlines the ways that the school will actively encourage attendance by promoting a positive school environment

❏ is based on accurate knowledge of the school's pattern of attendance

❏ reflects the characteristics of the school and its community

The policy also explains:

❏ parents' legal responsibilities

❏ how authorised and unauthorised absences will be categorised

❏ the criteria for granting authorised absence in special circumstances

❏ the procedures for parents when absence occurs

❏ the school's procedures when unauthorised absence occurs

❏ the school's procedures for referral to outside agencies

The policy is communicated in ways which will be easily understood by the school community.

Systems for the evaluation and revision of policy and practice are set up.

Conclusion

We have attempted in this booklet to provide a framework within which schools can understand their pattern of attendance and develop appropriate policies and practices for improving it.

Such attempts will need to be seen in the long, rather than the short-term, as dramatic overnight improvements are unlikely to occur. School communities also change over time, leading to possible changes in attendance patterns and the strategies necessary to deal with them. Efforts to improve attendance need to be regarded as an ongoing long-term commitment reflected in the school's overall development plan. We hope it is a commitment that you wish to make.

References

1. Barber, M. (1994) *Young people and their attitudes to school: An interim report of a research project.* Centre for successful schools: Keele University

2. Fogelman, K. (1978) School attendance, attainment and behaviour. *British Journal of Educational Psychology, 48(2),* 148-158

3. Hibbett, A. & Fogelman, K. (1990) Future lives of truants: Family formation and health related behaviour. *British Journal of Educational Psychology, 60,* 171-179

4. Hibbett, A. & Fogelman, K. (1990) Occupational outcomes of truancy. *British Journal of Educational Psychology, 60,* 23-36

5. Reynolds, D. (1987) School effectiveness and truancy. In K. Reid (1987) (Ed.) *Combating school absenteeism.* London: Hodder & Stoughton

6. Galloway, D. (1985) *Schools and persistent absentees.* Oxford: Pergamon

7. Elton Report (1988) *Committee of Enquiry into Behaviour and Discipline in Schools.* London: HMSO

8. University of North London Truancy Unit, Truancy Research Project (1994) *Truancy in English Secondary Schools: A Report for the DFE by the Truancy Research Project, 1991-1992, University of London Truancy Unit.* London: HMSO

9. Reid, K. (1985) *Truancy and school absenteeism.* London: Hodder & Stoughton

10. Reid, K. (1985) *Truancy and school absenteeism.* London: Hodder & Stoughton

11. Grimshaw, R.H. & Pratt, J.D. (1986) Counting the absent scholars: some implications for managerial practice arising from a survey of absenteeism in a city's secondary schools. *School organization, 6(1),* 155-173

12. Reid, K. (1986) Truancy and school absenteeism: The state of the art. *Maladjustment and therapeutic education, 4(3),* 4-17

13. Newson, J., Newson, E. & Barnes, P. (1977) *Perspectives on School at Seven Years Old.* London: Allen & Unwin

14. Apley, J. (1959) *The child with abdominal pains.* Oxford: Blackwell

15. Kennedy, W.A. (1965) School phobia: rapid treatment of 50 cases. *Journal of Abnormal Psychology, 70,* 285-298

16. University of North London Truancy Unit, Truancy Research Project (1994) *Truancy in English Secondary Schools: A Report for the DFE by the Truancy Research Project, 1991-1992, University of London Truancy Unit.* London: HMSO

17. Reid, K. (1986) Truancy and school absenteeism: The state of the art. *Maladjustment and therapeutic education, 4(3)*, 4-17

18. Reid, K. (1987) (Ed.) *Combating school absenteeism*. London: Hodder & Stoughton

19. Clwyd, A. (1994) *Children at risk: an analysis of illegal employment of children in Great Britain*. London: Labour Party

20. Clwyd, A. (1994) *Children at risk: an analysis of illegal employment of children in Great Britain*. London: Labour Party

21. University of North London Truancy Unit, Truancy Research Project (1994) *Truancy in English Secondary Schools: A Report for the DFE by the Truancy Research Project, 1991-1992, University of London Truancy Unit*. London: HMSO

22. Ames, C. (1992) Achievement goals and the classroom motivational climate. In D. Schunk & J. Meece. (Eds.) *Student perception in the classroom*. Lawrence Erlbaum

23. Epstein, J. (1989) Family structures and student motivation: A developmental perspective. In C. Ames & R. Ames (Eds.), *Research on motivation in education, Vol 3*. New York: Academic Press

24. University of North London Truancy Unit, Truancy Research Project (1994) *Truancy in English Secondary Schools: A Report for the DFE by the Truancy Research Project, 1991-1992, University of London Truancy Unit*. London: HMSO

25. Dearing, R. (1994) *The National Curriculum and its assessment: final report*. London: School Curriculum and Assessment Authority

26. West, D.J. (1982) *Delinquency; its roots, careers and prospects*. London: Heinemann

27. Carlen, P., Gleeson, D. & Wardlaugh, J. (1992) *Truancy: The politics of compulsory schooling*. Buckingham: Open University Press

Further reading and sources of information

Sources of information and help

Local sources include LEAs, universities, commercial providers of inservice training, and staff development co-ordinators. Information about national courses may be obtained from professional journals, papers and magazines.

In addition the following may be useful as providers of inservice training and general advice on truancy related issues.

University of North London Truancy Unit
School of Teaching Studies
University of North London
Tower Building
166-220 Holloway Rd,
London N7 8DB
Tel: 0171 607 2789

Leeds Attendance and Behaviour Project
(co-ordinators Peter Coster and Jo Walton)
Bramley Grange
Thorner, Leeds LS14 3DW
Tel: 0113 273 7716
This group can provide information on attendance issues and materials for inservice training.

National Council for Educational Technology
Milburn Hill Road
Science Park, Coventry CV4 7JJ
Tel: 01203 416994
NCET can provide advice on computerised registration packages.

Association of Chief Education Social Workers
Mrs Price, Room 431,
County Hall, Wakefield WF1 2QL
Tel: 01924 305519

Direct help in relation to provision for persistent absentees might be sought from:

Cities in Schools
60-1 Trafalgar Square, London WC2N 5DS
Tel: 0171 839 2899
Cities in Schools offer a range of services aimed at preventing or remedying pupils disaffection and truancy. Schemes include initiatives in primary and secondary schools, bridge courses for young people who have completely dropped out of school or been excluded, and summer schools providing educational and vocational courses in deprived areas during school holidays.

Local Education and Business Partnerships or local Training and Enterprise Councils (TEC) will have information on COMPACT, COMPACT PLUS and STEP schemes.

School Effectiveness and Improvement Centres
These provide consultancy services and inservice training in relation to school improvement.

Centre for Teacher and School Development
School of Education,
University of Nottingham,
University Park, Nottingham NG7 2RD
Tel: 0115 951 4496

Centre for Successful Schools
Department of Education
Keele University
Keele, Staffordshire ST5 5BG
Tel: 01782 621111

Improving the Quality of Education for All Project
Cambridge Institute of Education
Shaftsbury Rd, Cambridge CB2 2BX
Tel: 01223 369631

International School Effectiveness and Improvement Centre
Institute of Education
University of London
Bedford Way, London WC1H 0AL
Tel: 0171 612 6347

Centre for School Improvement
School of Education
University of Bath, BA2 7AY
Tel: 01225 826653

Centre for Research and Consultancy
Faculty of Education
University of Strathclyde
Jordanhill Campus
76 Southbrae Drive, Glasgow G13 1PP
Tel: 0141 950 3168/3369

Truancy
Booklets giving information about school attendance

Children out of school: a guide for parents and schools on non-attendance at school. London: Advisory Centre for Education

Education Observed 13: attendance at school. HM Inspectorate Publication

School Attendance: Policy and practice on categorisation of absence. London: Department of Education

Access, achievement and attendance in secondary schools. London: Office for Standards in Education

The challenge for education welfare. London: Office for Standards in Education

Haigh, G. (1993) *Using technology to combat truancy.* London: City Technology Colleges Trust Limited

Hallam, S. (1996) *Improving school attendance.* Oxford: Heinemann Educational

Learmouth, J. (1995) *More willingly to school? An independent evaluation of the truancy and disaffected pupils GEST programme.* A report prepared for the DFEE by an independent evaluation team led by James Learmouth. London: Department for Education and Employment

Lewis, E.J. (1995) *Truancy: the partnership approach.* Stoke on Trent: Smith Davis

MacBeath, J. (1995) The truancy file. University of Strathclyde: Quality in Education, Centre for Research and Consultancy
A resource pack for schools

Malcolm, H., Thorpe, G & Lowden, K. (1996) *Understanding truancy: links between attendance, truancy and performance.* Edinburgh: Scottish Council for Research in Education

Sutherland, A.E. (1995) *Persistent school absenteeism in Northern Ireland in 1992.* Belfast: NICER Research Unit

Available books raising issues related to truancy

Carlen, P., Gleeson, D. & Wardlaugh, J. (1992) *Truancy: The politics of compulsory schooling.* Buckingham: Open University Press

Le Riche, E. (1995) *Combating truancy in schools: listening to the voice of the pupil.* London: David Fulton in association with the Roehampton Institute

O'Keefe, D. J. (1993) *Truancy in English Secondary Schools.* London: HMSO

O'Keefe, D. J. & Stoll, P. (Eds) (1995) *Issues in school attendance and truancy.* Southport: Pearsons Professional

O'Keefe, D. J. & Stoll, P. (Eds) (1995) *School attendance and truancy: understanding and managing the problem.* London: Pitman Publishing

Whitney, B. (1994) *The truth about truancy.* London: Kogan Page

Bullying: Selected readings

Skinner, A (1992) *Bullying: An annotated bibliography of literature and resources.* Leicester: Youth Work Press/Calouste Gulbenkian Foundation (UK Branch)

Tattum, D. & Herbert, G. (1990) *Bullying: A positive response.* Cardiff: CIHE Learning Resources Centre

Sharp, S & Smith, P. (1994) *Tackling bullying in your school: a practical handbook for teachers.* London: Routledge

Bullying: don't suffer in silence: an anti-bullying pack for schools (1994). London: Department for Education

Maines, B. & Robinson, G. (1991) *The no blame approach to bullying.* Bristol: Lame Duck Publishing

Classroom practices: Selected readings

Bennett, N. & Dunne, E (1992) *Managing classroom groups.* Hemel Hempstead: Simon & Schuster

Dunne, R., & Wragg, T. (1994) *Effective teaching.* London: Routledge

Rogers, B. (1991) *You know the fair rule: strategies for making the hard job of discipline in school easier.* London: Longman

Wragg, E.C. (1993) *Class management.* London. Routledge

Useful addresses

National Association for Special Educational Needs
4/5 Amber Business Village
Amber Close, Amington,
Tamworth, Staffs B77 4RP
Tel: 01827 311500
This association publishes the following quarterly journals:
Support for Learning
British Journal of Special Education
Special!

Counselling: Selected readings

Hamblin, D.H. (1993) *The teacher and counselling.* Hemel Hempstead: Simon & Schuster

Bovair, K., & McLaughlin, C. (Eds.) (1993) *Counselling in schools.* London: David Fulton

Crompton, M. (1992) *Children and Counselling.* London: Edward Arnold

Galloway, D. (1990) *Pupils welfare and counselling: an approach to personal and social education across the curriculum.* London: Longman

Langham, M. & Parker, V. (1989) *Counselling skills for teachers.* Lancaster: Framework Press

Brammer, L.M. (1979) *The helping relationship: process and skills.* Englewood Cliffs: Prentice-Hall

Useful addresses

British Association of Counselling
1 Regent Place, Rugby CV21 2PJ
Tel: 01788 578328

National Association for Pastoral Care in Education (NAPCE)
c/o Department of Education
University of Warwick
Coventry CV4 7AL
Tel: 01203 523810
Publishes the *Journal of Pastoral Care in Education*

Training and Consultancy Ltd
22 Clarendon Place
Leeds LS2 9JY
Tel: 01132 334913
This unit provides inservice training, consultancy and research and evaluation services.

Children's Rights

Useful addresses

Advisory Centre for education
1B Aberdeen Studios
22 Highbury Grove
London N5 2DQ
Tel: 0171 354 8321
This centre provides information and advice on all aspects of education.

Children's Rights Office
235 Shaftsbury Avenue
London WC2H 8EL
Tel: 0171 240 4449
This unit aims to promote the fullest possible implementation of the UN Convention on the Rights of the Child, by monitoring progress on how far its principles and standards are met in the UK and raising awareness of the Convention's existence, its relevance, status and the government's responsibilities to implement it.

The Children's Legal Centre
University of Essex,
Wivenhoe Park,
Colchester CO4 3SQ
Advice Line: 01206 873820
Subscribers to Childright:
01206 872466
Publishes *Childright* - A bulletin of law and policy affecting children and young people in England and Wales.

Carers National Association
20-25 Glasshouse Yard
London EC1A 4JS
Tel: 0171 490 8818 (office),
0171 490 8898 (carer's line)
This association gives information about and for young carers.

Appendix

Categorising school absence as authorised or unauthorised

In this section we will give a brief resumé of the guidelines regarding school attendance presented in *School Attendance: Policy and practice on categorisation of absence* published by the DFE (1994). As the booklet makes clear, the guidelines do not constitute an authoritative interpretation of the law. That is exclusively a matter for the courts.

Parents' responsibilities: Parents and guardians are required to ensure that children of compulsory school age receive efficient full-time education. This means that they are responsible for ensuring that children attend and stay at school unless alternative arrangements for their education are made. They are also responsible for informing schools of any absence as soon as possible, ideally on the first day of absence. They should state the nature of the illness and when the child is expected to return to school.

How this contact is made should be decided by the school. Telephone calls, letters or personal contact are acceptable. The school should also state their attendance policy at parents' meetings, in the prospectus and at other opportunities, eg when letters are sent home.

Schools should ensure that parents are:

❏ reminded of their statutory duties

❏ aware of the schools' requirements as regards notification of absence

Registration: Schools, other than independent schools for boarders, must keep an attendance register on which at the **beginning** of each morning and afternoon session, pupils are marked present or absent. The absence must be registered as authorised or unauthorised.

Registers must be kept accurately as they may be used in evidence in cases where parents are being prosecuted for school attendance offences.

Where post-registration truancy is a problem, head teachers may wish to institute the taking of class registers at the beginning of each lesson.

The format of registers is left to individual schools, however, consistency of registration practice is vital. All teachers within the school must operate to the same rules.

Written registers must be kept in ink and corrections made in such a way that the original and the correction are both clearly visible. Corrections must also be distinguishable in computer systems and a printout must be made at least once a month. The printouts must be bound into annual volumes as soon as practicable after the end of the school year and retained for three years.

The education welfare system: LEAs are charged in law with enforcing school attendance. The LEA can apply to the courts for an education supervision order and, where necessary, they can prosecute the parents.

Schools should develop an effective working relationship with EWOs based on a clearly delineated division of labour.

LEAs should be informed of attendance problems. **All** schools must report to their LEA on continuous absences of not less than 2 weeks and on those pupils who fail to attend regularly, except where such absences are covered by a medical certificate.

Categorising absence: Parents can be prosecuted under the Education Act of 1993 for failing to ensure their child's attendance at school with the following exceptions:

❏ the pupil was absent with permission from an authorised person within school

❏ the pupil was ill or prevented from attending by an unavoidable cause

❏ the absence occurred on a day exclusively set aside for religious observance by the religious group to which the family belongs

❏ the school is not within walking distance of the home and no suitable arrangements have been made for transport to school, boarding accommodation or enabling the child to be registered at a school nearer his home

There are also some exceptions for the children of travellers.

Notes from parents: The school should specify the means of notifying absence. Only the **school** can approve absence not parents. The school does not have to accept the parents offered explanation as a valid reason for absence. If there are doubts about the explanation offered, or where there is no explanation, the absence must be treated as unauthorised.

Illness, medical and dental appointments: Such absences are considered authorised providing that the school is satisfied that the illness, appointments, etc are genuine.

Lateness: Schools should discourage lateness. Schools may keep their registers open for a reasonable time (recommended maximum 30 minutes). Where pupils miss registration and fail to provide an adequate explanation they should be marked as unauthorised absent for that session. If a person does arrive late and misses registration this must be noted for the purposes of emergency evacuation.

Minding the house/looking after brothers and sisters: This is an area where schools have discretion. The secretary of state would not expect schools to grant leave except in exceptional circumstances. Most cases will be **unauthorised absence**.

Shopping during school hours: It is highly unlikely that such absence can ever be justified.

Special occasions: It is for the school to determine whether an absence in this category should be authorised or not. It will clearly depend on the circumstances.

Family bereavements: Schools should respond sensitively to requests for leave of absence to attend funerals or associated events. They have discretion to authorise such absences. Where a pupil is absent for more than the agreed period early contact should be made with the family.

Family holidays and extended trips overseas: There is discretionary power for leave to be granted for the purpose of an annual family holiday or a holiday during term time. Only in exceptional circumstances may the amount of leave granted exceed two weeks. No parent can demand leave of absence for the purposes of a holiday. Periods of more than two weeks are considered as exceptional. Where holidays of more than two weeks are planned to visit overseas relatives the school may find it helpful to discuss with the parents the best timing for the trip from an educational point of view.

Days of religious observance: An offence is not committed where the absence results from participation in a day set aside exclusively for religious observance by the religious body to which the parents belong.

Traveller children: Travellers are protected from prosecution if they can show that the nature of their trade requires travel from place to place and that the child has attended school as regularly as possible. Also where the child has attained the age of 6 years and has made at least 200 attendances during the previous 12 months.

Interviews: Where a child attends a job interview or application for a place at an institution of further or higher education the school has discretion to authorise the absence. Schools should expect and ask for advance notification.

Work experience and public performances: Leave of absence may be granted for work experience or to participate in approved public performance. If the student is then absent from the work experience or performance this will constitute unauthorised absence.

Off-site activities: These fall into two categories, school directed, eg educational visits and individual activities, eg music examinations. School activities will normally be registered as absent. Where a small group is involved and not at the place of normal registration such absences will be classed as authorised.

Where the activity is of a more individual nature the school can authorise absence at its discretion. If a registered pupil requires special off-site tuition leave of absence may be granted and the absence treated as authorised.

Excluded pupils: Where a pupil has been temporarily excluded he or she should remain on the school roll. This should be treated as authorised absence. If a pupil has been excluded permanently his absence should be treated as authorised until after review. Once the exclusion is confirmed he or she should be struck off the school roll.

Pupils at pupil referral units: Off-site units are required to keep attendance records. Provision is made for dual registration to facilitate return to mainstream. The pupil must be classified as authorised absent when he or she is not attending. Arrangements of this kind need to be formalised in writing.

Study leave: Only year 11 pupils should be granted study leave. It should be granted sparingly, normally with a maximum of two weeks.

School leaving date: Pupils are required to remain at school until the relevant leaving date. Any absence not agreed in advance must be treated as unauthorised.

KEY POINTS

❏ Registered pupils of compulsory school age are required by law to be in school.

❏ The aim of schools should be to expect regular attendance, even when schools recognise the problems of individual families and children.

❏ Lateness should be discouraged.

❏ Where a pupil is absent without prior permission an explanation is required. If one is not forthcoming the absence must be treated as unauthorised.

❏ Schools are not obliged to accept parental notes where there is reasonable doubt as to the validity of the explanation.

❏ Explanations such as minding the house, looking after children, shopping, etc will not normally be accepted as reasons for absence.

❏ Parents should not expect, as of right, that schools will agree to family holidays in term time. Each application must be considered on its merits.

❏ Even where absence is authorised schools should be ,alert to emerging patterns of absence which may seriously disrupt continuity of learning.

❏ In promoting regular attendance schools should work closely with education welfare officers.